Did Y

WEST

A MIS

GW00392129

Compiled by Julia Skinner

With particular reference to the work of Martin Andrew
and Nick Channer

THE FRANCIS FRITH COLLECTION

www.francisfrith.com

First published in the United Kingdom in 2012 by The Francis Frith Collection®

This edition published exclusively for Bradwell Books in 2012
For trade enquiries see: www.bradwellbooks.com or tel: 0800 834 920
ISBN 978-1-84589-688-1

Text and Design copyright The Francis Frith Collection®
Photographs copyright The Francis Frith Collection® except where indicated.

The Frith® photographs and the Frith® logo are reproduced under licence from
Heritage Photographic Resources Ltd, the owners of the Frith® archive and trademarks.
'The Francis Frith Collection', 'Francis Frith' and 'Frith' are registered trademarks of
Heritage Photographic Resources Ltd.

All rights reserved. No photograph in this publication may be sold to a third party other than in the original
form of this publication, or framed for sale to a third party. No parts of this publication may be reproduced,
stored in a retrieval system, or transmitted, in any form, or by any means, electronic, mechanical, photocopying,
recording or otherwise, without the prior permission of the publishers and copyright holder.

British Library Cataloguing in Publication Data

Did You Know? West Sussex - A Miscellany
Compiled by Julia Skinner
With particular reference to the work of Martin Andrew and Nick Channer

The Francis Frith Collection
Oakley Business Park,
Wylye Road, Dinton,
Wiltshire SP3 5EU
Tel: +44 (0) 1722 716 376
Email: info@francisfrith.co.uk
www.francisfrith.com

Printed and bound in Malaysia
Contains material sourced from responsibly managed forests

Front Cover: **COCKING, THE CHURCH 1906** 54384p
Frontispiece: **WARNHAM, THE VILLAGE SHOP 1928** 80849x
Contents: **FERNHURST, THE CROSSROADS 1908** 59671

The colour-tinting is for illustrative purposes only, and is not intended to be historically accurate

AS WITH ANY HISTORICAL DATABASE, THE FRANCIS FRITH ARCHIVE IS CONSTANTLY BEING
CORRECTED AND IMPROVED, AND THE PUBLISHERS WOULD WELCOME INFORMATION ON
OMISSIONS OR INACCURACIES

CONTENTS

INTRODUCTION

'The great hills of the South Country
They stand along the sea;
And it's there walking in the high woods
That I could wish to be…'

From 'The South Country' by Hilaire Belloc (1870-1953)

The modern county of West Sussex was created in 1974, when the ancient county of Sussex was divided into two new counties, East and West Sussex. This division gave East Sussex the venerable county town of Lewes, and compensated West Sussex with the ancient cathedral city of Chichester as its county town. 72 years before that division was made, in 1902, the writer Hilaire Belloc walked across the county, from Robertsbridge in the east to South Harting in the west, a journey of some 90 miles; he recorded his impressions of rural Sussex during his odyssey in his book 'The Four Men', first published in 1912. Hilaire Belloc fell in love with Sussex and not long afterwards he settled at Shipley, south of Horsham; he stayed there for the rest of his life, and celebrated his adopted county in both poetry and prose. Many of the photographs of West Sussex in this book were taken around the same time as Belloc made his epic walk. Some of the locations seem to have changed little over the years, particularly in the rural areas and quiet villages, but others seem like a different world. Parts of the coast have altered beyond recognition since the Frith photographers captured classic seaside scenes at Bognor, Worthing and Littlehampton, and now a chain of urban development extends all the way from Shoreham-on-Sea to Chichester. Busy roads have replaced quiet country lanes, and traffic now thunders through what used to be sleepy towns that only burst into life on market or fair days.

Despite the changes that have taken place in West Sussex over the years, this still remains a beautiful county of delightful villages, quaint churches, historic, picturesque timber-framed cottages, handsome country houses, romantic castles and magnificent scenery. If you climb Black Down near Fernhurst, in the north west corner of the county close to the Surrey border, the view from this highest point in West Sussex is still much as it was when the Victorian Poet Laureate Alfred, Lord Tennyson (1809-1892) used to walk there from his home nearby, at Aldworth House. This was one of his favourite spots, and he famously described the view from Black Down in his 'Prologue to General Hamley':

> *'You came, and looked and loved the view,*
> *Long-known and loved by me,*
> *Green Sussex, fading into blue*
> *With one gray glimpse of sea.'*

SOUTH HARTING, THE SHIP INN 1906 54415

WEST SUSSEX DIALECT
WORDS AND PHRASES

'Ackle' – to work out correctly.

'All of a loop' – disordered.

'Along-of' – because of, on account of.

'Balk' – a straight path through a ploughed field.

'Chacket' – cough.

'Chog' or 'shog' – an apple core.

'Grummut' – an awkward or difficult boy.

'Juggy wren' – the name for a male wren, one of Britain's smallest bird, with **'Jenny wren'** being a female wren.

'Let be how it will' – an expression always pronounced as one word, as **'Letbehow'twill'**, meaning 'Let the consequences be what they will'; often abbreviated in West Sussex into **'behowtel'**.

'Picksome' – fastidious, or fussy.

'Runagate' – a tramp.

'Twitten' – a narrow path or alleyway between buildings.

'Vlothered' – agitated, flustered, stressed out, hot and bothered.

HAUNTED WEST SUSSEX

There are said to be many haunted locations around West Sussex. Here are just a few:

The Roman town of Noviomagus Regnensium lies below modern Chichester. The defensive stone walls around the old Roman town were refaced and rebuilt in the Middle Ages, and in the 18th century were adapted into rampart walks along much of the northern half of the city, which still survive. The ghost of a Roman soldier is reputed to walk the boundary of the ancient city walls at night. He is also said to pop into the Chichester Inn in West Street occasionally, although only the top portion of his body is visible; his appearance is always accompanied by a noticeable drop in temperature.

The old coaching inn formerly called the George Hotel in Crawley's pedestianised High Street (now the Ramada Crawley Gatwick Hotel) is said to be haunted by the ghost of Mark Hewton, a night porter who liked to deliver wine to guests in the evening, regardless of whether they wanted it or not. Any wine left he would consume himself. Unfortunately for him, one guest put poison in some of this wine, which Hewton drank and promptly died. Staff at the hotel have reported feeling uncomfortable in the locality of his room, now number seven, and some have said they have seen strange, indistinct shapes there. They also have trouble with the corridor lights near the room, which frequently turn themselves on and off.

The ruins of Bramber Castle, north of Worthing are reputed to be haunted by three pitiful ghostly children, said to be Blanche, Jane and Hugh, the youngest offspring of William de Braose, 4th Lord of Bramber who was in discord with bad King John in the early 13th century. The story goes that the children were taken hostage by King John and allowed to starve to death at Windsor Castle. Their pitiful shades are said to roam around the remains of their family home, holding out their hands as if begging for food…

WEST SUSSEX MISCELLANY

The Romans began their conquest of Britain in AD43, and their administration of the country lasted until the early 5th century. In the first century AD they built a military road linking London with the Roman town of Noviomagus Regnensium, at what is now modern Chichester. The road later became known as Stane Street ('stane' meaning 'paved with stone'), and the straight stretch of the A29 between Billingshurst and Pulborough follows its line. A length of that Roman road can still be found running through Eartham Wood, just east of the A285 between Chichester and Petworth, then a bridle path follows it for three miles over the downs to Bignor Hill. Bignor itself is the site of the excavated remains of an impressive Roman villa. The huge site, which is open to the public, is famous for its splendid mosaic floors; subjects depicted in the floors include a head of Medusa in the bath suite, an evocative portrayal of the four seasons, Venus with cherub gladiators, and Zeus, king of the Roman gods, depicted as an eagle.

BILLINGSHURST, CHURCH CAUSEWAY 1912 64881

FISHBOURNE, THE ROMAN PALACE, A MOSIAC FLOOR c1968
F132002

The most famous Roman site in West Sussex is the excavated remains of the palace at Fishbourne, near Chichester, which was probably an important administrative centre. Fishbourne Palace was the most impressive building in Roman Britain, an opulent, luxurious residence with an extensive underfloor hypocaust system (hot air central heating) and magnificent mosaic floors. The floor pictured here has a centrepiece of a winged cupid riding a dolphin, surrounded by sea panthers and sea horses. Fishbourne Palace was probably originally built in the first century AD for Tiberius Claudius Cogidubnus, King of the Regnenses, the local British tribe, who appears to have been a firm ally of the Romans; the Roman town of Noviomagus Regnensium lies beneath modern Chichester, and the inscription on an ancient stone tablet found in Chichester in 1723 records that a temple to Neptune and Minerva was erected there by permission of Tiberius Claudius Cogidubnus, who bore the title of 'rex et legatus Augusti in Britannia' – 'King and Legate to the Roman Emperor in Britain'. The inscribed stone is now set into the outside wall of the Assembly Rooms in North Street in Chichester.

BYWORTH, THE VILLAGE 1906 54367

From the 5th century onwards, Saxon migrants began to settle along the wide river estuaries and numerous tidal creeks of Sussex that were very similar to their flooded homelands on the north German and Frisian coasts. Over the next few centuries the Saxon settlements of initial family communities evolved into today's coastal plain hamlets, villages and towns, many of which have names that betray their Saxon origins. The ending '-ing' meant 'belonging to a family or tribe', thus Worthing was 'the place of Wurht's People'. The ending '-ton' denoted an enclosure which developed into a village. Other derivations are: '-ham', meaning 'a hamlet'; '-stead', '-stock' or 'stoke', which mean 'a place'; '-worth', meaning an enclosure; '-ley' or '-holt', meaning 'a wood'; '-den', meaning 'a valley' or 'a clearing for grazing animals'; and 'fold', meaning 'a clearing in a dense forest'. It was also these people who gave the old county of Sussex its name, which meant 'the land of the South Saxons', recorded in the 'Anglo-Saxon Chronicle' as 'Suoseaxe'.

Christianity arrived later in Sussex than in many other parts of Britain, for it was not until AD681 that Wilfrid, Bishop of York (later canonised as St Wilfrid) came to the region from Northumbria on his evangelising mission to convert the South Saxon people. St Wilfrid arrived at Selsey and established a monastery there, which later became a cathedral and the seat of the Anglo-Saxon bishopric of Sussex. At the time of the Norman Conquest of 1066 Selsey was a much larger town than today, with many important buildings, but that town and its cathedral succumbed to coastal erosion and was swallowed by the sea, hence the local legend of a cathedral under the sea; this caused the bishopric's seat to be moved from Selsey to Chichester in 1075.

SELSEY, THE LIFEBOAT HOUSE c1965 S91326

The late struggle between Christianity and paganism may be the reason for the abundance of legends and customs about the Devil in Sussex. Many sites are associated with tales of the Devil, which often show him being outwitted by canny Sussex people. One of the most famous is linked with the Devil's Dyke, a spectacular deep combe, or cleft, in the Dyke Hills near Fulking, north-west of Brighton. According to Sussex legend, the Devil was so infuriated by the Christian piety of Sussex people that he began to dig the Dyke to the sea in an attempt to flood the area with sea water and destroy the churches of the Weald. His plot was foiled by an old woman who rushed up the hill with a lighted candle held behind a sieve, which fooled a cockerel into thinking it was dawn and made it crow. Hearing the cockerel crow, and thinking that the sun was about to rise, the Devil abandoned his task and fled, for he cannot bear sunlight.

Another Sussex tradition refers to the north door of churches as 'the Devil's door', and there are several possible explanations for this. One is that the north door was where the villagers who were still pagan would enter a church that had been built on an old pagan site, so they could continue their own practices on a site that still had relevance to them. Another theory is that the north door was left open when a baby was being baptised, so the departing spirit of the Devil could exit after being commanded to leave the child by the Christian rite, and the door would then be hurriedly closed after the ceremony, to prevent the Devil coming back – the churches of St Nicholas at Worth, on the eastern outskirts of Crawley (one of the finest Saxon churches in the country) and St Giles at Horsted Keynes, south of East Grinstead, are particularly associated with this custom. Yet another theory is that people believed the Devil lurked outside the north door, waiting to catch the souls of unwary people who used it, and that it was quite unsafe to use this exit. Whatever the reason, the association of north doors of churches with the Devil was so strong that most of them have now been blocked up.

Bosham (pronounced Bozzam) lies at the end of a tidal inlet on the eastern edge of Chichester Harbour. King Canute, who ruled England between 1016 and 1035, had a palace here, and Bosham is traditionally the place where he tried to command the incoming tide to go back, to demonstrate to his fawning courtiers that he was not all-powerful as they suggested.

Bosham's church features in the Bayeux Tapestry that chronicles the events of the Norman Conquest of England in 1066. In 1064 the Anglo-Saxon nobleman Harold Godwinson, Earl of Wessex set out on a sea voyage from Bosham, and the tapestry shows him entering Bosham's church to pray for a safe journey before embarking. Despite his prayers, he was shipwrecked and fell into the hands of Duke William of Normandy. William made Harold swear an oath of allegiance to him, promising to uphold William's claim to the English throne when Edward the Confessor died – it was Harold's failure to do so, and his acceptance of the throne himself, that led to William invading England and King Harold's death at the Battle of Hastings.

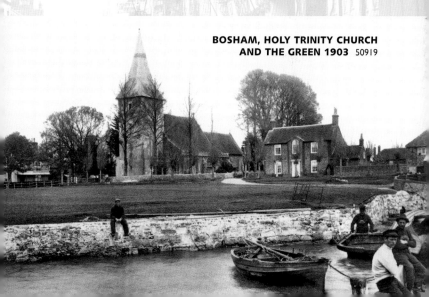

BOSHAM, HOLY TRINITY CHURCH AND THE GREEN 1903 50919

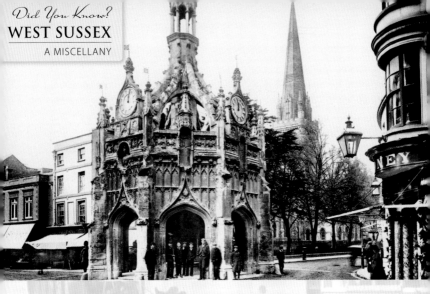

CHICHESTER, THE MARKET CROSS AND THE CATHEDRAL 1903 50923

Chichester's superb medieval Market Cross in the city centre was erected by Bishop Storey in 1501 so that poor people could sell their goods there free of market tolls. One of the niches on the Cross holds a bronze bust of Charles I, installed there in 1669 after his son, Charles II, was restored to the throne, as a judicious mark of Chichester's loyalty – the city's Member of Parliament, William Cawley, had been a signatory on the death warrant of Charles I at the end of the Civil War. Cawley fled the country after Charles II came to the throne and lived abroad for the rest of his life, but his name lives on in Chichester in the Cawley almshouses in Broyle Road, which he endowed.

An important industry of medieval Chichester was needlemaking. Names recorded of people living in the town in the 13th century (le Nedeler and le Aguiller) show that the industry was established at an early date. The last recorded needleworker in Chichester was working in 1783. The industry is remembered in the name of The Needlemakers, the road between the former needlemakers' area of St Pancras and The Hornet.

Chichester's cathedral was started in the late 11th century by Bishop Ralph de Luffa, and in the main it is still a Norman building, with later additions. The spire of the cathedral spire collapsed in 1861, fulfilling a prophecy in an old rhyme that said 'If Chichester tower do fall, in England there's no King at all'. There was indeed no King, for Queen Victoria was on the throne at the time. The collapsed spire was rebuilt under the supervision of Sir George Gilbert Scott, who added 6 feet to its height.

Chichester Cathedral is the only medieval cathedral in Europe to have a separate bell tower – its massive, detached bell tower was built between about 1375 and 1440 to carry the bells because the cathedral's central tower had become too weak to allow them to be rung.

In 1929, two 12th-century panels of Purbeck stone carved with scenes depicting the biblical story of the raising of Lazarus from the dead were found built into the eastern piers of the crossing of the cathedral. They were re-erected in the south aisle of the choir, and are considered to be among the greatest works of Romanesque monumental sculpture in England. More recent artworks of note in this magnificent building include a dazzling modern altar tapestry by John Piper, a stained-glass window by Marc Chagall, and a painting by Graham Sutherland of Christ appearing to the Virgin Mary on the first Easter morning.

One of the tombs in Chichester Cathedral is of Richard FitzAlan, Earl of Arundel (1313–1376), and his second wife, Eleanor of Lancaster (1318–1372). The effigies of the earl and his wife are represented hand in hand. This tomb inspired Philip Larkin to write one of his best-known poems, 'An Arundel Tomb', published in 1964, which begins 'Side by side, their faces blurred, The earl and countess lie in stone', and ends with the famous line 'What will survive of us is love'.

An important archaeological site of the Lower Palaeolithic period of prehistory is at Boxgrove Quarry, north of Chichester, where the fossilised human remains of 'Homo heidelbergenis' have been discovered; at some 500,000 years old, these are amongst the oldest hominid remains ever discovered in Europe. The nearby village of Boxgrove is famous for its church, formerly part of Boxgrove Priory. When the priory was dissolved by Henry VIII in 1536 the Lord of the Manor, Thomas West, 9th Lord de la Warr, saved its church from demolition so that its magnificent nave could be used as the village's parish church. He was also responsible for its beautifully decorated ceiling, commissioning local artist Lambert Barnard (1485-1567) of Chichester to paint it with the arms and crests of his own and his wife's families, entwined with flowers and foliage. Inside the church is the chantry chapel where monks prayed for the souls of the de la Warr family dead, its stonework ornately carved with grotesque monsters, naked men and a Dance of Death ('danse macabre'). Chantry chapels were abolished in 1547 and this is the only complete chantry chapel surviving in the whole of Sussex.

The old RAF airfield at Tangmere played an important role during the Battle of Britain of the Second World War; the Tangmere wing of Fighter Command was commanded by the legendary legless fighter ace Group Captain Douglas Bader, who is commemorated in the name of the village pub. Tangmere was also where SOE agents left for secret operations in occupied France aboard 'Black Lysander' flights. The airfield is now home to the Tangmere Military Aviation Museum, where equipment used by those special agents can be seen. The airfield holds an important place in aviation history as it was home to the world speed record-breaking aircraft of the High Speed Flight in the post-war years, and the Hawker Hunter plane in which Neville Duke flew from Tagmere in 1953 and broke the world air speed record can also be seen there.

Over 50 buildings of architectural or historic interest can be visited at the Weald and Downland Open Air Museum at Singleton, between Chichester and Midhurst. The buildings date from the 13th to the 19th centuries and were all threatened with destruction on their original sites. They were dismantled, conserved and re-erected at the museum, where they form an important record of the vernacular buildings of south-east England.

BOXGROVE, THE CHURCH, THE DE LA WARR CHANTRY 1899 44892

**MIDHURST, OLD MARKET HOUSE AND THE SPREAD EAGLE HOTEL
1923** 73641

Midhurst is a delightful town of ancient timber buildings and picturesque narrow lanes. A local custom is that a Curfew Bell is rung at 8pm every evening at the town's parish church of St Mary Magdalene and St Denys. According to tradition, many centuries ago a traveller got lost outside the town as darkness fell; he managed to reach Midhurst and safety by following the sound of its church bell tolling the nightly curfew that signalled the time for all household fires to be doused, to reduce the risk of the town burning down overnight. In gratitude, the traveller bought a quarter-acre piece of land in Knockhundred Row (later known as Curfew Garden) and gave it to Midhurst to use the income raised from it to keep the bell tolling – that income still pays for the bellringer, the repair of the bell, and the maintenance of the church tower and belfry, and the Curfew Bell has continued to ring in Midhurst every night, except for the years of the Second World War.

On the outskirts of Midhurst is Cowdray Park, set around the ruins of Cowdray House. In 1542 this magnificent Tudor mansion was inherited by Sir Anthony Browne; in 1548 it passed to his son who became the 1st Viscount Montague, and remained the Montague family home for centuries. Before inheriting Cowdray, Sir Anthony had acquired Battle Abbey in East Sussex, following its dissolution by Henry VIII, which he converted into a grand house. According to legend, the last monk to leave the abbey cursed Sir Anthony with the words 'By fire and water thy line shall come to an end, and it shall perish out of the land'. The prophecy appeared to have come true when the 8th Viscount Montague drowned in the Rhine in 1793, the same year that Cowdray House was destroyed by fire, and the last two sons of the Montague dynasty drowned in a boating accident in 1815; the house was never rebuilt.

One of the most ancient oak trees in the country stands in Cowdray Park. It may be as much as 1,000 years old, and is called Queen Elizabeth's Oak because in 1591 the 1st Lord Montague entertained Queen Elizabeth I and her court for a week at Cowdray, and the queen took shelter from a storm beneath its branches whilst hunting in the park.

MIDHURST, COWDRAY PARK, QUEEN ELIZABETH'S OAK 1921 70202

Trotton is a small village west of Midhurst that has an exceptional medieval wall painting in its parish church of St George. The artwork dates from the late 14th century and depicts the Last Judgment as described in Matthew 25:31–46. In the centre of the painting is Jesus Christ; beneath him is Moses, on his left is the 'Spiritual Man' surrounded by the Seven Acts of Mercy (clothing the naked, feeding the hungry, giving drink to the thirsty, tending the sick, receiving the stranger, visiting the prisoner, and burying the dead) and on his right is the 'Carnal Man' surrounded by the Seven Deadly Sins (pride, gluttony, anger, avarice, lust, sloth and envy). This church is also notable for wall paintings depicting the Camoys family, the medieval lords of the manor, as well as a number of tombs of members of that family. One of the finest is the table-tomb in the middle of the chancel, where the ornate, well-preserved brass memorial on the tomb depicts Thomas de Camoys, 1st Baron Camoys, who fought at the battle of Agincourt in 1415, holding hands with his second wife, Lady Elizabeth Mortimer – she was formerly married to Sir Henry Percy, better known as 'Harry Hotspur', and was poetically immortalised as 'Gentle Kate' in William Shakespeare's play 'Henry IV, Part 1'. The small figure at her knee on the brass represents her stepson Richard Camoys, who died in infancy. Another important memorial brass in the nave of the church commemorates Margaret de Camois, who died in 1310 – this is the oldest known brass of a woman in England, and shows Margaret wearing a wimple and long gown, with a small dog sleeping at her feet.

The Seven Deadly Sins also feature in the church of St Peter and St Paul at Linchmere, in the extreme north-west corner of the county east of Liphook. Inside the church on the north wall is an unusual piece of sculpture of seven monks representing the seven vices. The work dates from about 1300, and was carved from hard volcanic rock, inset with the monks' faces carved from marble. It is not hard to guess which of the monks represents Sloth – six of them are clean-shaven, but Sloth has a beard and droopy moustache, and is obviously too lazy to set to work with a razor!

The beautiful 17th-century mansion of Uppark stands high on the downs above South Harting, west of Midhurst. It was devastated by fire in 1989 but has since been restored. The servants' quarters are shown as they were in the late 19th century when Uppark's housekeeper was the mother of the author H G Wells. After his victory at the Battle of Waterloo in 1815, the Duke of Wellington was offered a country estate of his own by a grateful nation. He originally asked for Uppark, but when he went to view it the duke reckoned that the steep hill and drive to the house would wear out his horses, necessitating constant replacement, and chose Stratfield Saye in Hampshire instead.

Another of West Sussex's great houses is Petworth, east of Midhurst. The late 17th-century mansion was designed by the French architect Daniel Marot, with the gardens laid out by 'Capability' Brown in the 18th century. A frequent visitor to Petworth in the 1830s was the painter J M W Turner, who drew inspiration from the house and grounds and began to develop the brilliant interweaving of light and colour that characterised the last phase of his work. He had a studio in the Old Library above the Chapel, and a number of his pictures still hang there. Other paintings in the art collection of Petworth House include work by Holbein, Rembrandt, Hals, Van Dyck, Gainsborough and Reynolds.

PETWORTH, THE HOUSE 1898 42839

Petworth is a place of narrow lanes, half-timbered Tudor houses and Georgian buildings, including the arcaded 18th-century town hall in the Market Place and the Somerset Hospital in North Street, established in 1746 by the Duke of Somerset to provide homes for twelve poor widows. The Petworth Cottage Museum at 346 High Street is a recreation of when the house was occupied by Mrs Mary Cummings, who worked as a seamstress for Lord Leconfield at Petworth House in the early 20th century; the house is furnished as it might have been in 1910, with a workroom set up as a sewing room. St Mary's Church in Petworth looks very different now from how it is seen in this photograph – the spire was added in 1827, but demolished in 1947. In front of the church in this view is the distinctive lamp standard designed by Sir Charles Barry, the joint architect of the Houses of Parliament who also restored St Mary's Church in Petworth in the 1820s. It was erected in 1851 as a token of thanks to Lord Leconfield of Petworth House, who provided the town with gas lighting, and remains a landmark in the town.

PETWORTH, EAST STREET 1906 54362

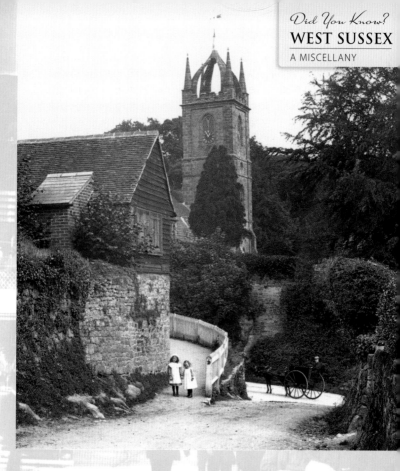

TILLINGTON, ALL HALLOWS CHURCH 1912 64899

An interesting West Sussex church is All Hallows Church at Tillington, one mile west of Petworth. The coronet design of the church tower is the only one of its kind in West or East Sussex, and is rarely found throughout the whole country. The early 19th-century design is distinguished by flying buttresses at the four corners, meeting in a finial and forming a Scots crown. The architect is unknown.

On the A272 north-east of Petworth is Wisborough Green. There was a thriving glass-making industry in this part of West Sussex in medieval times, which intensified after 1567 with the arrival of Huguenot (Protestant) glass-makers fleeing religious persecution in France, who brought improved techniques to the area. There is a commemorative window in Wisborough Green's church to some of those Huguenot glass-workers, constructed with locally-made glass from around 1600. However, the glass-making furnaces were in direct competition with the Sussex iron industry (see page 41) for coppiced wood from the area for fuel; in 1615 Parliament decided the iron industry was more important because of its military uses and made it illegal to use wood to fuel the glass furnaces, which soon brought the local glass-making industry to an end.

Close to Wisborough Green is Kirdford, which was also a glass-making centre in the past, as recalled in the name of Glasshouse Lane and the village sign, which incorporates a piece of old local glass. Set into the wall of the old rectory near the church in the centre of the village is a stone plaque inscribed with a dire warning about the evils of alcohol. One story says it was erected by villagers as a warning to their local cleric, who they thought was over-fond of the demon drink, but another says it was put there in 1850 by the then Vicar of Kirdford, the Reverend J F Cole, as a warning to his parishioners.

Temperance was also a feature of a religious group known as The Society of Dependents that used to live in several communities around this area of West Sussex. They were nicknamed 'Cokelers' because of their consumption of cocoa instead of alcohol. The group was founded by John Sirgood at Loxwood in 1850 and by the time he died in 1885 the congregation numbered around 2,000 members, with communities in Wisborough Green, Kirdford, Northchapel, Lurgashall, Warnham and Upper Norwood. At several places where the Cokelers set up chapels they also established village stores, called 'Combination Stores', that were the joint property of the local congregation, although non-members were welcome to shop there. The Society of Dependents community has now died out, but the chapel they built in 1869 at Spy Lane in their headquarters of Loxwood is still there, and is now the Emmanuel Fellowship Chapel.

KIRDFORD, THE VICAR'S WARNING c1955 K118019

Degradation of Drunkenness

There is no sin which doth more deface God's image than drunkenness, it disguiseth a person and doth even unman him Drunkenness makes him have the throat of a fish, the belly of a swine, and the head of an ass. Drunkenness is the shame of nature, the extinguisher of reason, the shipwreck of chastity and the murderer of conscience. Drunkenness is hurtful to the body the cup kills more than the cannon, it causes dropsies, catarrhs, apoplexies, it fills the eye with fire, and the legs with water and turns the body into an hospital.

The River Arun is the longest river in West or East Sussex. It rises in St Leonard's Forest east of Horsham, then flows through the centre of West Sussex, meandering south from Pulborough and cutting through the South Downs past Arundel to empty into the sea at Littlehampton. The river is tidal as far inland as the disused Pallingham Quay near Pulborough. Stopham Bridge, over the River Arun just west of Pulborough, is one of the finest medieval bridges in the country, and carried the traffic of the A283 road until a new bridge was built beside it in the 1980s. It was built in the early 15th century and six of the arches are in their original medieval form, but the central arch was raised in 1822 to allow masted barges to pass below the bridge.

Just outside Pulborough on the A29 road is Hardham, whose ancient church contains medieval wall paintings (more accurately frescos) of national importance. The depth of colour in the paintings and their fine state of preservation is exceptional. Subjects depicted include the Nativity, Passion and Resurrection, the parable of Dives and Lazarus and a portrait of Adam and Eve on the point of temptation in the Garden of Eden. The paintings are part of the so-called Lewes Group, believed to have been produced by a workshop associated with Lewes Priory in East Sussex. (The other three churches in the Lewes Group, with magnificent medieval wall paintings, are at Coombes, a largely Norman church north of Lancing, Clayton, north of Brighton, and Plumpton, north-west of Lewes in East Sussex.)

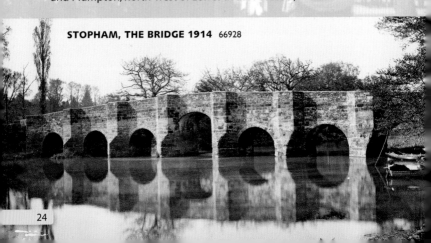

STOPHAM, THE BRIDGE 1914 66928

ARUNDEL, THE CASTLE 1906 56725

Arundel lies on the tidal reaches of the River Arun and was once a flourishing port. The town is dominated by its spectacular castle, the principal seat of the Dukes of Norfolk since 1580, when the 4th Duke of Norfolk married the last of the Fitzalan line who had owned the castle and Earldom of Arundel since 1243. The first castle was built there in the late 11th century by Roger Montgomery, Earl of Shrewsbury, to guard the gap in the South Downs cut by the River Arun and defend the Arun valley against sea raiders, but little of the earliest phase of the castle remains – just the motte (or enditched mound) of 1068 and the gatehouse of 1070. In the late 19th century the 15th Duke of Norfolk employed the architect Charles Alban Buckler to 'restore' the building by constructing him a medieval-style castle, so most of what we see today is Victorian mock medieval. Arundel Castle's extraordinary Gothic skyline of towers and battlements is believed to have been the inspiration for the fantastical castle in Mervyn Peake's series of 'Gormenghast' novels; the author could see the castle from his rented home at Warningcamp where he lived whilst writing the first novel in the series, 'Titus Groan'.

Burpham (pronounced 'Burfam') is a picturesque village east of Arundel that is named after the Saxon 'burh', or fortification, which was built on a hill above the village to defend the River Arun against attack by the Vikings. The massive figure-of-eight enclosure is the most notable Saxon fortification in the whole of Sussex. A good view of the northern ramparts of the fortification can be seen by the George & Dragon pub in the village. Burpham is also famous for its 12th-century church, which contains a leper's window through which the wretched victims of this terrible disease could watch services and be blessed by the priest, who remained inside the church.

The village of Walberton, south-west of Arundel, is famous for three macabre 18th-century gravestones in St Mary's churchyard which are carved with scenes depicting their victims' causes of death. The best-preserved example, although the earliest, commemorates the death in 1767 of Charles Cook. The intricately-carved gravestone shows, in rich detail, Charles Cook lying crushed beneath a fallen tree, watched by a hat-wearing man holding an axe, who raises his hand in horror; to the left is a laughing skeleton, and to the right is Old Father Time carrying his traditional scythe and hourglass, and above the whole scene is a company of trumpet-playing angels presided over by God, who is depicted holding a book and pen and surrounded by the clouds of heaven.

South of Walberton is the village of Yapton, a short distance from the coast north of Middleton-on-Sea. 'Were you born in Yapton?' is a Sussex saying for when someone has forgotten to close a door. It is believed to derive from the 18th century, when smuggling was widespread along the Sussex coast – it was a local practice to leave doors in Yapton open or unlocked so smugglers could hide their goods in the houses if they were being pursued by the excise men.

BOGNOR REGIS, THE BEACH 1890 22625

Bognor Regis began as a Saxon village recorded in AD680 as 'Bucgan ora', meaning 'Bucge's shore' or 'Bucge's landing place'. In the late 18th century Sir Richard Hotham bought much land in the area and started developing it into a 'desirable sea-bathing resort' that he re-named 'Hothamton', but by 1830 the name of the town had reverted back to Bognor. 'Regis' was added to its name in 1929 after George V recuperated at nearby Aldwick after an illness. Bognor's growth as a popular resort only really got going when a station opened at Woodgate in 1845, followed by a branch line into the centre of the town in 1862. Bognor's pier came in 1865, one of the earliest piers in Sussex. The pier now survives in a drastically truncated form: the seaward part was destroyed by storms in the 1960s, a further section disappeared in 1999, and another 18 metres (60 feet) of the pier was removed in 2008 following storm damage. Bognor's pier is the venue for the annual 'International Bognor Birdman' competition for human-powered 'flying' machines, an entertaining event held each summer. Contestants launch themselves from the end of the pier in a variety of inventive and outlandish flying contraptions, and the prize goes to the one who glides the furthest distance.

27

'Away to sweet Felpham, for heaven is there', wrote the poet and painter William Blake (1757-1827) in wistful mood in a letter to a friend, Mrs Flaxman, in 1808. Blake lived between 1800 and 1803 at Felpham, just east of Bognor, in what is now Blake's Cottage in Blake's Road – the house is now marked by a commemorative plaque. Blake wrote of his time there that 'Sussex is certainly a happy place; and Felpham in particular is the sweetest spot on earth. Heaven opens here on all sides its golden gates…'. It was whilst he lived at Felpham that William Blake wrote his epic poem 'Milton', which contains the famous lines about 'England's green and pleasant land', inspired by the Sussex countryside, that were later set to music as the hymn 'Jerusalem' by Sir Hubert Parry (1848-1918), who lived a few miles along the coast at Rustington, near Littlehampton.

LITTLEHAMPTON, THE HARBOUR 1903 50218

LITTLEHAMPTON, SOUTH TERRACE 1890 22665

Littlehampton is where the River Arun meets the sea. There were two Littlehamptons, a busy port and fishing village about half a mile inland on the east bank of the Arun, although not much of it survives nowadays, and the fashionable seaside resort which grew up after 1800, with its seafront and neighbouring streets lined with handsome Georgian and Victorian villas, such as those seen in photograph 22665 of South Terrace (above). The older Littlehampton was a thriving port in the Middle Ages, when stone from Normandy was landed there for the construction of many of the churches and castles of Sussex. In photograph 50218, on the opposite page, the photographer looks north-west along the east bank wharves towards the site of the swing bridge that opened in 1908, five years after this view, and has now been rebuilt as well as superseded by a road bridge further north. A famous modern landmark of Littlehampton is the East Beach Café, a distinctive fully-welded monocoque structure on the seafront described by its designers, Heatherwick Studio, as resembling 'a piece of weathered flotsam swept up onto the beach'. Local opinion is divided on its merits – some people see it as an eyesore, whilst others consider it to be a world-class piece of modernistic architecture.

HIGH SALVINGTON, THE OLD MILL 1919 68994

On the Downs north of Ferring is Highdown Hill. On its summit is the Miller's Tomb, which local miller John Olliver had built there in 1763 – some 27 years before his death in 1793! Local legend says John Olliver was also the leader of a local band of smugglers, and used the tomb to store contraband, as well as using his windmill on Highdown Hill to signal to smugglers out at sea, setting the sails at different angles to indicate whether excise men were in the area. The windmill on Highdown Hill was demolished in 1826, but another mill still stands in the area, at High Salvington, 3 miles north of Worthing. This is a fine old Sussex downland 'post and socket' mill with a domesticated structure enclosing the trestle. Powered by two common cloth sails, the mill was suspended on a post and turned into the wind by means of a tailpole. High Salvington dates back to about 1750 and was the first mill in England to be insured against fire – flour is highly combustible, and mills were very prone to catching fire and burning down. This view shows the mill when the site was used as a tea garden. It is now restored to working order, with an original-style roundhouse enclosing the trestle, and open to visitors.

A few miles east of High Salvington is another distinctive West Sussex church, at Sompting, between Worthing and Lancing. The Saxon church of St Mary has a distinctive and very unusual cap on its tower known as a 'Rhenish Helm', a four-sided pyramidal cap of shingled gables. This design is quite common in the Rhineland of Germany, hence its name, but the Sompting example is unique in Britain.

Broadwater, a northern suburb of Worthing, is centred around a large grassy area known as Broadwater Green. Not far away, on the verge where Broadwater Street West meets the Grove Lodge A27 roundabout, stands the hollowed, truncated (but still living) remnant of an old oak tree known as The Midsummer Oak, so called because there was an old tradition that on Midsummer's Eve (June 23rd) skeletons would rise from beneath the tree and dance around it, hand in hand, until they heard the first cock crow at sunrise the following day, when they would sink back into the ground. The oak tree was threatened with felling in 2006 but was saved by a local campaign; its rescue is celebrated each year with a meeting around the tree at midnight on Midsummer's Eve.

SOMPTING, THE CHURCH 1890 22735A

Worthing began to grow into a popular resort in the late 18th century and is now the largest seaside town in West Sussex. Worthing's pier was the first pleasure pier in the whole of Sussex when it opened in 1862, and it remains the oldest surviving pier of both West and East Sussex. A further attraction for the resort's visitors opened in 1910 in the building known as The Dome, the prominent building in the background of this view. This was originally built as a 'Kursaal', a German name for an assembly building in spa and seaside towns used for concerts and other entertainments. The Dome housed a roller-skating rink on the ground floor, with a concert hall on the first floor. In 1921 the skating rink was converted into Worthing's first permanent cinema. The Dome narrowly escaped demolition in the 1980s, but is now recognised as one of Worthing's important buildings. Under the auspices of The Worthing Dome & Regeneration Trust it has been restored to its full glory as a stunning example of an Edwardian entertainment complex, and The Dome is still in use as a cinema for the town.

WORTHING, THE DOME FROM THE PIER ENTRANCE 1921 71455

A number of early 19th-century houses away from the seafront of Worthing have unusual porches surrounding their front doors which are known as 'boat porches' because of their shape – the porches have ogee-headed roofs which resemble the hulls of fishing boats. The design is thought to derive from the local fishermen's custom of using upturned boats to make shelters over their doorways. These 'boat porches' are an architectural feature unique to Worthing. Examples can be seen in Warwick Place and Portland Road.

One of the 19th-century visitors who came to Worthing was the playwright Oscar Wilde – a plaque at Esplanade Court on The Esplanade marks the site of the house where he stayed in the summer of 1894. It was whilst staying there that he wrote perhaps his best-known play, 'The Importance of Being Earnest', inspired by an article he read in the 'Worthing Gazette' about an abandoned baby being found in a hamper at King's Cross Station in London. Wilde commemorated Worthing's part in what he described as 'the best play I have ever written' by giving the name 'Jack Worthing' to the hero of his play.

East of Lancing, south of the A27 road between Brighton and Worthing, is Shoreham Airport, also known as Shoreham (Brighton City) Airport. The airport opened in 1911 as the Brighton and Shoreham Aerodrome, and is the oldest licensed airfield in Britain still in operation. The Terminal Building of what was then known as the Brighton, Hove and Worthing Municipal Airport opened in 1936 and is still in use at the airport. Designed by Stavers H Tiltman, the Grade II listed building is an architectural triumph of Art Deco. It has been used as a location for several period films and television programmes, including 'Agatha Christie's Poirot', starring David Suchet.

SHOREHAM-BY-SEA, THE CROWN AND ANCHOR HOTEL c1950 S123019

Shoreham-by-Sea is sited near the mouth of the River Adur at the eastern end of the West Sussex coast. The earliest settlement here was what is now Old Shoreham, based around the partly Anglo-Saxon church of St Nicholas, but the silting up of the river estuary caused a new settlement and harbour to be established further downriver in the early 12th century. The superb Romanesque church of St Mary de Haura of 'New Shoreham' dates from this time – its name means 'St Mary of the Haven, or Harbour'. The church was originally much larger, but what remains is still impressive, especially the great choir. The church is full of wonderfully detailed medieval carved stonework, including three 'Green Men' on the ceiling of the south chancel aisle.

A landmark of Shoreham's High Street is the giant effigy of a pirate that stands in the prow of a boat fixed to the frontage of the Crown and Anchor pub. The figure was placed there in 1931, and was carved from Canadian teak by master carver Francis John McGinnity in his Brighton studio.

The River Adur was formerly navigable for large vessels up as far as Steyning, where there was once a large and busy port; however the silting up of the river valley in the 14th century left Steyning's harbour inaccessible to shipping and the river little more than a stream. The focus of the town shifted southwards from around the church and became centred on the junction of Church Street and the High Street, and Steyning became a market town. The centre of Steyning includes rows of picturesque gabled houses and period buildings. The tall, three-storeyed building with an arched doorway in the centre of this view is the original gateway to the Grammar School at Steyning, which was founded in the 16th century and endowed by William Holland in 1614 to ensure its future; a past pupil of the school was the mathematician John Pell (1611-85). Amongst other things, John Pell gave his name to Pell's Equation (the indeterminate quadratic equation $y2 = nx2 + 1$) as well as inventing the arithmetical division sign: $\div$.

STEYNING, CHURCH STREET, THE GRAMMAR SCHOOL c1955 S192020

In the 1070s a castle was built at Bramber, to protect the port of Steyning and the local area, which gave its name to one of the administrative areas known as 'Rapes' that Sussex was divided into in the Middle Ages. Each rape had a strip of coast, an area of downland for cultivation, and a strip of Wealden forest to the north. As well as the Rape of Bramber, the other six Rapes of Sussex were Chichester, Arundel, Lewes, Pevensey and Hastings. Bramber's castle has all but disappeared now – just a fragment of masonry survives on the castle mound. Bramber's church of St Nicholas was originally built as the chapel for Bramber Castle, and is the oldest post-conquest Norman church in West and East Sussex. Another historic building in Bramber is the 15th-century timber-framed St Mary's House. This splendid building contains the unique 'Painted Room', the earliest example of three-dimensional trompe l'oeil painting in England, which was decorated like this for a visit of Queen Elizabeth I to the house in the 16th century.

A short distance east of Bramber is the village of Upper Beeding, nesting against the hills. Confusingly, Upper Beeding is lower geographically than its namesake, Lower Beeding, which lies about 15 miles away near Horsham!

BRAMBER, THE PAINTED ROOM, ST MARY'S c1960 B179044

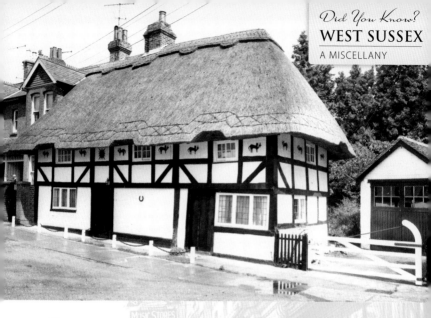

HENFIELD, PINCHNOSE GREEN, THE CAT HOUSE c1960 H313108

At the junction of the A2037 from Upper Beeding and the A281 from Horsham is Henfield. A famous building in the village is The Cat House at Pinchnose Green (so called because of the smells produced by a tannery that used to be located in this area), opposite the junction of Martyn Close with Church Street. This picturesque thatched cottage is decorated with a frieze of cut-out metal cats below the roofline, with each cat holding a bird in its paws. In the 19th century this was the home of the local joiner, Mr Ward, who was most upset when his pet canary was killed by a cat belonging to the Canon Nathaniel Woodard (the founder of Lancing, Ardingly and Hurstpierpoint Colleges), who lived nearby, at Martyn Lodge in Church Street. Mr Ward took his revenge on Canon Woodward by installing various contraptions in his garden, including cut-out metal cats, attached to a long thread strung with bells that he jangled whenever Canon Woodward walked past the house as a reminder of the crime his cat had committed. Those metal cats now adorn the upper storey of the house.

Until the 19th century the town centre of Burgess Hill was an area known as St John's Common where an important livestock fair was held each summer. It was the enclosing of the commons of the area in 1828 and 1855 that began the development of Burgess Hill, but the town's growth was really triggered by the arrival of the London to Brighton Railway in 1841. The name of the area of Burgess Hill called World's End is believed to have originated from the railway navigators constructing the section of the line between Haywards Heath and Clayton. They lived in temporary shanty towns whilst they were constructing railway lines all around the country and regarded the district just north of Burgess Hill as the most remote they had ever settled in; someone amongst them dubbed it 'The End of the World', or 'World's End', and the name is still in use today.

In 1830 Haywards Heath was described as 'a byword for the wilderness of its aspect, the rusticity of its few and scattered cottages, and the miryness of its roads'. The arrival of the railway in 1841 helped development of the town, which grew even more rapidly after 1862 when its heath, or common, was enclosed and the land was used for residential development. Many of the original villas of the Victorian town of Haywards Heath have now gone, to be replaced by modern blocks of flats, but St Wilfrid's Church still stands in the town, built in the 1860s on the former site of a windmill; inside this distinguished Wealden sandstone building are some stained glass windows, dated 1867, which were designed and executed by William Morris, famous for his associations with the Pre-Raphaelite Brotherhood and English Arts and Crafts Movement.

Muster Green in Haywards Heath is so called because it was used as a mustering place for militia after the restoration of Charles II to the throne in 1660. It was probably in this area that the 'Battle of Haywards Heath' took place in 1642, during the Civil War, when a Royalist force was defeated by Parliamentarians. The skirmish is recalled with the representations of a Cavalier and Parliamentary soldier on the town sign of Haywards Heath. Between them is the round-headed rampion flower, known as the 'Pride of Sussex'.

**HAYWARDS HEATH
THE RIVER OUSE
RAILWAY VIADUCT
2005** H252702

The Sussex Lunatic Asylum was built at Haywards Heath in the
1850s, later known as St Francis Hospital. The hospital's first medical
superintendent was Charles Lockhart Robertson, who pioneered the
humane treatment of mentally ill patients there. He focused on the
positive, encouraged his patients to take part in activities such as
gardening, and refused to allow them to be viewed as figures of ridicule.
This was a radical way of dealing with mentally ill patients at the time, but
Robertson's methods gradually came to be acknowledged and accepted
by the wider medical profession. Changes to mental health legislation
in the 1970s and 80s caused St Francis Hospital to become redundant.
Part of its site was used to build the Princess Royal Hospital, and its
main building (now called Southdowns Park) has been converted into
residential apartments.

A magnificent monument to the men who built the London to Brighton
Railway is the River Ouse Railway Viaduct, north of Haywards Heath. This
engineering and architectural masterpiece was designed by John Rastrick
and built by 6,000 labourers between 1839 and 1841, using 11 million
bricks. The viaduct carries the railway line across the River Ouse valley on
a series of 37 arches. The attractive pavilions at each end were designed
by David Mocatta, a student of the great architect Sir John Soane.

East Grinstead was founded in the early 13th century as a medieval 'new town'. No houses from the earliest town survive, but a number from the 14th and 15th centuries still stand along the High Street in one of the longest stretches of medieval buildings in the country. The Sackville family, the Earls of Dorset, owned most of East Grinstead for centuries, and Cantelupe Road is named after the title of the eldest son of the family. Sackville College at the eastern end of the High Street was endowed as an almshouse in 1608 by Robert Sackville, 2nd Earl of Dorset, and still serves that function today. The Warden of Sackville College from 1846 until his death in 1866 was the Reverend John Mason Neale, who was a noted hymnologist – his best-known work is probably the Christmas carol 'Good King Wenceslas', written at East Grinstead in 1854.

It was at the Queen Victoria Hospital in East Grinstead that the renowned plastic surgeon Archibald McIndoe performed reconstructive surgery on badly burned airmen who had received severe hand and facial injuries during the Second World War. The types of planes flown by the airmen treated there are recalled in the names of roads opposite the hospital, Lancaster Drive, Blenheim Close and Merlin Way.

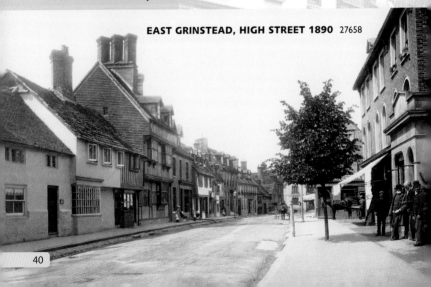

EAST GRINSTEAD, HIGH STREET 1890 27658

The 18th-century mansion called East Court in College Lane in East Grinstead is a listed building that now houses the Town Council. In 1884 the line of longitude which passes through Greenwich Observatory in south-east London was chosen as the prime meridian, dividing east from west. East Grinstead also lies on this line and a plaque marking its position is set into the terrace behind East Court. There, as at Greenwich, it is possible to stand with one foot in the eastern hemisphere and the other in the western! To mark the Millennium in 2000, every street in East Grinstead that the meridian crosses was marked with a special marker stone, set into the kerb, verge or edge of a footpath.

140 million years ago, the ridge on which East Grinstead is built was covered by a large freshwater lake in which were millions of tiny snails. As the snails died they fell to the bottom and eventually fossilized to form shelly limestone. When this material is polished it resembles marble and was used, as such, in the 18th and 19th centuries when it was known as 'Sussex marble' or 'winklestone'.

The deposits of iron ore in the sandstones of the Weald caused an important iron industry to flourish in Sussex in the past, which pre-dated the smelting of iron using coal. The fuel used was charcoal, made by coppicing trees in the local woods and forests. The introduction of water-powered bloomery forges in the 15th century revolutionised the industry, and Sussex became the 'black country' of 16th- and 17th-century England. Furnaces and forges were sited beside streams whose water was diverted and contained by dams to create furnace ponds to drive waterwheels powering the furnace bellows, and hammer ponds that stored water to drive waterwheels powering huge forging hammers used for working the iron. However, coal-fired blast furnaces were introduced in the mid 18th-century, making iron production easier and cheaper, and the iron industry moved to the north of England, to be nearer the supply of coal. All that is left now of this once-important industry are some of the old furnace and hammer ponds created to power the workings – although many are now dry, those that remain form beautiful features of the landscape, and there are a number of old hammer ponds around East Grinstead, Horsham and Crawley.

CRAWLEY, THE HIGH STREET AND THE GEORGE HOTEL 1905 53313

Crawley was a major iron smelting settlement in medieval and Tudor times, and in the 18th and early 19th centuries its position along the London to Brighton road made it an important and prosperous coaching town. Although Crawley has grown and changed almost beyond recognition since this photograph was taken, some elements of the historic old town remain, including what used to be called the George Hotel but is now (2012) the Ramada Crawley Gatwick Hotel, a former coaching inn in the High Street, with its distinctive 'gallows sign' projecting out from the building. In past times condemned felons were hanged in front of the inn; whilst awaiting execution, they were held in a windowless cell that still exists in the Brewery Shades pub in the High Street.

At the junction of Crawley's High Street with the Boulevard is the original Manor House for the town, known for many years as Crawley Place. The oldest parts of the property date from the 1320s, which makes it Crawley's oldest house, although many of its timbers are now hidden behind more modern brick walls and roof. A very large and old elm tree used to stand outside the house, which led to it being called The Tree House, or simply The Tree. Though the elm tree is long gone, the building is still known by that name. Another old building used to stand behind The Tree, known as 'Crawley Barn'. In the late 1960s, when the site was being redeveloped, the barn was recognised as being Crawley's early Moot (meeting) Hall; this important 15th-century building was taken down and re-erected in the Weald and Downland Open Air Museum at Singleton, north of Chichester (see page 14), where it is called the Upper Hall and used as the museum's library and meeting place.

Crawley was designated a New Town in 1947 which gave it a new, modern town centre and massive housing development. Queen's Square was the planned centre of the New Town, and was officially opened in 1958. Originally there was an admired fountain in Queen's Square in the shape of a boy with a dolphin, but it proved difficult to keep vandal-proof and is now safely sited behind glass in a courtyard at the Town Hall. In the early days there was also an unusual tall clock in Queen's Square, seen in the photograph of Queen's Square on page 49, which marked the hours by chiming the tune from the film 'Genevieve' whilst model cars moved around its middle, celebrating the fact that the London to Brighton Veteran Car Run passed through the town each November. The clock mechanism was probably too exposed and proved expensive to upkeep, and was eventually sold off.

HORSHAM, THE CAUSEWAY, CAUSEWAY HOUSE 1901 58194

Horsham was founded by Saxon farmers, its name meaning 'a place of horses' or 'a horse settlement'. The area from the River Arun up the Causeway to the Carfax represents the oldest part of Horsham, centred around St Mary's Church. The church has a broach spire that is twisted out of alignment to the south-east, probably due to the use of unseasoned timber in its construction, which has warped over the centuries. This photograph shows Causeway House in The Causeway, a picturesque late-Tudor building that is now the home of Horsham Museum. Amongst its interesting displays is a replica of the 'pentacycle', the brainchild of local architect and inventor Edward Burstow in the 19th century. Cashing in on the new-found concept of the bicycle, he thought his innovative five-wheeled contraption would be just the thing for postmen with heavy bags of letters. It had one large central wheel with four smaller wheels set squarely around it for stability, earning it the nickname of the 'hen and chickens'. This eccentric extension of the pennyfarthing was given trials by the Post Office in 1882, but they came to nothing, and Burstow's pentacycle never saw the production line.

The Carfax is the open space which has been at the heart of the old town of Horsham since at least medieval times. Its name first appeared in 1524 as 'Skarfolkes', probably a corruption from the French meaning 'the meeting of four ways'. It was originally common land used as shared pasture by the local villagers; gradually the homesteads of the developing town spread around and surrounded the space, which then became the site for the town's markets and fairs. The fountain on the right of this photograph was erected in 1897 to commemorate the Diamond Jubilee of Queen Victoria; it has now been relocated to North Street. The tall, elegant spire seen in the background of this view is of the 19th-century St Mark's Church. The body of this church was demolished in 1989 to make room for modern development, but its spired tower was left to stand in what is now St Mark's Court, where it remains as a lone and rather incongruous survivor of Victorian Horsham amid the 21st-century town, dwarfed by the modern offices of the Royal and Sun Alliance Insurance Group.

HORSHAM, THE CARFAX 1907 58192

SPORTING WEST SUSSEX

Horse-racing on the Downs at Goodwood, near Chichester, was started in 1802 by the Duke of Richmond and Gordon of Goodwood House. This beautiful horse-shoe shaped course with its spectacular views across the Downs to the sea, nicknamed 'Glorious Goodwood', soon became established, and since 1814 the five-day meeting every July has been a popular social occasion as well as a key event in the flat-racing calendar. Amongst other events, Goodwood racecourse hosts two of the UK's 31 Group One flat races, the Sussex Stakes and the Nassau Stakes. When Ascot Racecourse commemorated the accession of Edward VII in 1901 with the building of a new grandstand, the Duke of Richmond responded by building an imposing two-tier grandstand at Goodwood, which was completed by 1904. This photograph shows it in use in its first year.

Cowdray Park near Midhurst is regarded as the home of British Polo, which has been played on the Cowdray estate for over 100 years – the first competitive event took place there in 1910. Around 450 polo matches are played at Cowdray each season, with the major event being the Veuve Clicquot Gold Cup for the British Open Championships.

GOODWOOD, THE RACECOURSE 1904 52291

Another important 'horsey' sporting venue in West Sussex is the All England Jumping Course at Hickstead, west of Burgess Hill, which was the first permanent showground for equestrian sport in the country when it opened in 1960. The course hosts a number of international events but is probably best-known for its showjumping activities. Amongst other events, the course hosts the four-day British Jumping Derby Meeting in June, but it is also the venue for the Royal International Horse Show each July, the official horse show of the British Horse Society, which includes other events besides showjumping.

Stoolball is an ancient game that originated in Sussex in the 15th century and is played at local league level by a number of stoolball clubs in West Sussex. It is played mainly by women and is similar to cricket. The two wickets, square boards 4 feet (1.22 metres) off the ground, are defended using round bats. Its name seems to come from its origins as a game played by milkmaids who used their milking stools as bats with another bat hung in a hedge or from a tree as the wicket. Despite its early origins, stoolball was only officially recognised as a sport by the Sports Council in 2008.

MIDHURST, POLO AT COWDRAY PARK c1960 M74058

QUIZ QUESTIONS

Answers on page 52.

1. What is the traditional nickname for inhabitants of Arundel?

2. Why is it that many houses and cottages in Midhurst have woodwork painted bright yellow, as well as in the surrounding villages, such as Cocking?

3. What are known as 'Primrose', 'Stepney' and 'Bluebell', and whereabouts in West Sussex can you find them?

4. Which sport is linked with the Ebernoe Horn Fair which takes place every year on St James's Day, July 25th, at Ebernoe, about 5 miles north of Petworth, near the A283 road?

5. Rome is famous for the magnificent painted ceiling of the Sistine Chapel in the Apostolic Palace, the official residence of the Pope in the Vatican City, painted by Michelangelo between 1508 and 1512. However, you can also see the painted ceiling in West Sussex – how so?

ARUNDEL, HIGH STREET
1902 48792

48

CRAWLEY, QUEEN'S SQUARE c1965 C182196

6. Which species of tree used to be so common in Sussex that it was nicknamed 'the Sussex Weed'?

7. Tinsley Green, in the Borough of Crawley, in the extreme north of the county close to the border with Surrey, is where the British Championships take place each year for which activity?

8. In the old Sussex dialect, what would you be if someone described you as 'nunty'?

9. The photograph on this page shows Queen's Square in Crawley as it looked in the mid 1960s. The tall clock seen in this view is now gone, but a feature of the square that is still there today is the bandstand – what is the connection between that bandstand and the famous Grand National horserace?

10. Whereabouts in Sussex can you find Jack and Jill?

RECIPES

CHICHESTER PUDDING

Chichester Pudding is a bread pudding which is almost like a soufflé. It should be served as soon as it comes out of the oven or, like a soufflé, it will collapse. Serves 4.

> 4 slices of good quality white bread,
>   with the crusts removed
> 15g/ ½ oz butter
> 2 eggs, separated
> 2 tablespoonfuls of caster sugar
> 250ml/9 fl oz milk
> Grated rind and the juice of 1 large lemon

Pre-heat the oven to 180°C/350°F/Gas Mark 4.

Use the butter to grease a 600ml (1 pint) soufflé or deep-sided ovenproof dish.

Crumble the bread to form coarse breadcrumbs.

Beat the egg yolks with the sugar and then beat in the milk. Add the breadcrumbs, lemon juice and lemon rind. Whisk the egg whites until they are stiff and stand in peaks, then carefully fold them into the mixture. Turn the mixture into the prepared dish, and immediately place towards the top of the pre-heated oven.

Bake for 35-40 minutes until the pudding is well-risen and set, and has turned golden. Serve straight away.

SUFFOLK APPLE CAKE

Sussex was once renowned for the quality of its apples, and there are a number of local varieties such as the Five Crowns of Sussex, the Sussex Duck's Bill, the Sussex Mother, the Crawley Beauty, the Goodwood Pippin, the Petworth Nonpareil and the Egremont Russet, thought to have been raised by Lord Egremont in the 1870s on the Petworth estate. This recipe for the delicious apple cake differs from apple cakes made in other areas as it includes walnuts and has a layer of grated apples in the middle.

> 225g/8oz butter or margarine, softened to room temperature
> 225g/8oz dark soft brown sugar
> 3 large eggs, beaten
> 150g/5oz finely chopped walnuts
> 150g/5oz sultanas or raisins, or a mixture of both
> 225g/8oz self-raising flour
>   (either white or sifted wholemeal flour work well)
> 450g/1 lb cooking apples, peeled, cored and grated
> Half a teaspoonful ground cloves, or ground cinnamon if preferred

Pre-heat the oven to 180°C/350°F/Gas Mark 4 and grease and line a cake tin 22-24cms (8-9 inches) in diameter. Beat together the softened butter or margarine and 175g/6oz of the sugar until light and fluffy. Gradually add the beaten eggs, a little at a time, beating well after each addition and adding a small amount of the flour if necessary, to prevent the mixture curdling. Reserve one tablespoonful of the chopped walnuts and use a large metal spoon to fold the rest into the mixture, together with the dried fruit and the flour, mixing gently but thoroughly so that is all well combined. Pour half the mixture into the prepared cake tin. Mix the ground cloves, or cinnamon, into the grated apples, and spread the apples over the cake mixture in the tin. Cover with the remaining cake mixture, spreading and levelling it gently to form an even surface. Mix together the remaining sugar and chopped walnuts to make a topping, and sprinkle the mixture evenly over the surface of the cake. Bake just below the centre of the pre-heated oven for 1¼-1½ hours, until the top is caramelized but not over-browned. Remove from the oven and leave to cool in the tin for 30 minutes, then turn out the cake onto a wire rack, remove the lining paper and leave to cool completely.

QUIZ ANSWERS

1. A traditional nickname for people born in Arundel is 'Mullets', after the grey mullets that are caught in the River Arun that flows through the town.

2. This yellow paintwork identifies houses and cottages that are part of the Cowdray Park Estate, which owns property all around the Midhurst area. The decision to use yellow was made by the 2nd Viscount Cowdray, Weetman Harold Miller Pearson, when he inherited the Cowdray estate in 1927. As he sat as a Liberal Member of Parliament (for Eye in Suffolk), he chose yellow as that is the colour of the Liberal Party. The custom of using 'Cowdray Yellow' on the estate has remained to this day, although it is no longer making a political statement!

3. These are the names of some of the locomotives that run on the Bluebell Line, a preserved steam railway that runs through the countryside of the north-eastern corner of West Sussex. When the first section of the line was opened for business by the Bluebell Railway Preservation Society in 1960, this was England's first standard gauge passenger-carrying preserved steam railway.

4. Cricket. The Ebernoe Horn Fair is held on the village common, with the main event being a cricket match between Ebernoe and a nearby village. At the end of the day the highest scoring batsman in the match is presented with a set of horns taken from a sheep that has been roasted during the day and which is eaten as part of the event.

5. An exact replica of the Sistine Ceiling can be found in the Roman Catholic Church of the English Martyrs in Goring-by-Sea, near Worthing – and at 30 feet nearer the ground than the original ceiling in Rome, it is much easier to see! The ceiling was painted

over five years by local parishioner Gary Bevans, who completed the work in 1993. This spectacular artwork is the only full-sized copy of the Sistine Ceiling in the world.

6. Oak trees.

7. Tinsley Green is famous as the venue for the British Marbles Championships, which are held outside the Greyhound Inn every Good Friday. The event is said to date back to 1600 when two local men were in competition for the affections of a girl in the village and decided which of them would woo her by playing a game of marbles.

8. 'Nunty' is an old Sussex dialect word meaning sulky, or moody.

9. The bandstand in Queen's Square in Crawley was originally sited at Gatwick Racecourse, north of the town, which opened 1891 and remained in use until 1940. The bandstand was moved to Crawley in the late 1950s when the expansion of Gatwick Airport took over the former racecourse land. In 1915, 1916 and 1917, during the First World War, the Grand National was held at Gatwick Racecourse, the Aintree course having been requisitioned by the War Office – the rider of the 1917 Grand National winner there was Lester Piggott's grandfather, Ernie Piggott.

10. On the Downs above Clayton, north of Brighton, are two 19th-century windmills known as the Jack and Jill Windmills. Jack is a large brick-built tower mill with four patent sails and was winded by a five blade fantail; Jill is a timber post mill with four patent sails and is winded by a five blade fantail mounted on the tailpole. The tower mill Jack is conserved, whilst the white post mill Jill is in full working order and open to visitors most Sundays between May and September

FRANCIS FRITH

PIONEER VICTORIAN PHOTOGRAPHER

Francis Frith, founder of the world-famous photographic archive, was a complex and multi-talented man. A devout Quaker and a highly successful Victorian businessman, he was philosophical by nature and pioneering in outlook. By 1855 he had already established a wholesale grocery business in Liverpool, and sold it for the astonishing sum of £200,000, which is the equivalent today of over £15,000,000. Now in his thirties, and captivated by the new science of photography, Frith set out on a series of pioneering journeys up the Nile and to the Near East.

INTRIGUE AND EXPLORATION

He was the first photographer to venture beyond the sixth cataract of the Nile. Africa was still the mysterious 'Dark Continent', and Stanley and Livingstone's historic meeting was a decade into the future. The conditions for picture taking confound belief. He laboured for hours in his wicker dark-room in the sweltering heat of the desert, while the volatile chemicals fizzed dangerously in their trays. Back in London he exhibited his photographs and was 'rapturously cheered' by members of the Royal Society. His reputation as a photographer was made overnight.

VENTURE OF A LIFE-TIME

By the 1870s the railways had threaded their way across the country, and Bank Holidays and half-day Saturdays had been made obligatory by Act of Parliament. All of a sudden the working man and his family were able to enjoy days out, take holidays, and see a little more of the world.

With typical business acumen, Francis Frith foresaw that these new tourists would enjoy having souvenirs to commemorate their days out. For the next thirty years he travelled the country by train and by pony and trap, producing fine photographs of seaside resorts and beauty spots that were keenly bought by millions of Victorians. These prints were painstakingly pasted into family albums and pored over during the dark nights of winter, rekindling precious memories of summer excursions. Frith's studio was soon supplying retail shops all over the country, and by 1890 F Frith & Co had become the greatest specialist photographic publishing company in the world, with over 2,000 sales outlets, and pioneered the picture postcard.

FRANCIS FRITH'S LEGACY

Francis Frith had died in 1898 at his villa in Cannes, his great project still growing. By 1970 the archive he created contained over a third of a million pictures showing 7,000 British towns and villages.

Frith's legacy to us today is of immense significance and value, for the magnificent archive of evocative photographs he created provides a unique record of change in the cities, towns and villages throughout Britain over a century and more. Frith and his fellow studio photographers revisited locations many times down the years to update their views, compiling for us an enthralling and colourful pageant of British life and character.

We are fortunate that Frith was dedicated to recording the minutiae of everyday life. For it is this sheer wealth of visual data, the painstaking chronicle of changes in dress, transport, street layouts, buildings, housing and landscape that captivates us so much today, offering us a powerful link with the past and with the lives of our ancestors.

Computers have now made it possible for Frith's many thousands of images to be accessed almost instantly. The archive offers every one of us an opportunity to examine the places where we and our families have lived and worked down the years. Its images, depicting our shared past, are now bringing pleasure and enlightenment to millions around the world a century and more after his death.

For further information visit: www.francisfrith.com

INTERIOR DECORATION

Frith's photographs can be seen framed and as giant wall murals in thousands of pubs, restaurants, hotels, banks, retail stores and other public buildings throughout Britain. These provide interesting and attractive décor, generating strong local interest and acting as a powerful reminder of gentler days in our increasingly busy and frenetic world.

FRITH PRODUCTS

All Frith photographs are available as prints and posters in a variety of different sizes and styles. In the UK we also offer a range of other gift and stationery products illustrated with Frith photographs, although many of these are not available for delivery outside the UK – see our web site for more information on the products available for delivery in your country.

THE INTERNET

Over 100,000 photographs of Britain can be viewed and purchased on the Frith web site. The web site also includes memories and reminiscences contributed by our customers, who have personal knowledge of localities and of the people and properties depicted in Frith photographs. If you wish to learn more about a specific town or village you may find these reminiscences fascinating to browse. Why not add your own comments if you think they would be of interest to others? See **www.francisfrith.com**

PLEASE HELP US BRING FRITH'S PHOTOGRAPHS TO LIFE

Our authors do their best to recount the history of the places they write about. They give insights into how particular towns and villages developed, they describe the architecture of streets and buildings, and they discuss the lives of famous people who lived there. But however knowledgeable our authors are, the story they tell is necessarily incomplete.

Frith's photographs are so much more than plain historical documents. They are living proofs of the flow of human life down the generations. They show real people at real moments in history; and each of those people is the son or daughter of someone, the brother or sister, aunt or uncle, grandfather or grandmother of someone else. All of them lived, worked and played in the streets depicted in Frith's photographs.

We would be grateful if you would give us your insights into the places shown in our photographs: the streets and buildings, the shops, businesses and industries. Post your memories of life in those streets on the Frith website: what it was like growing up there, who ran the local shop and what shopping was like years ago; if your workplace is shown tell us about your working day and what the building is used for now. Read other visitors' memories and reconnect with your shared local history and heritage. With your help more and more Frith photographs can be brought to life, and vital memories preserved for posterity, and for the benefit of historians in the future.

Wherever possible, we will try to include some of your comments in future editions of our books. Moreover, if you spot errors in dates, titles or other facts, please let us know, because our archive records are not always completely accurate—they rely on 140 years of human endeavour and hand-compiled records. You can email us using the contact form on the website.

Thank you!

For further information, trade, or author enquiries
please contact us at the address below:

**The Francis Frith Collection, Oakley Business Park,
Wylye Road, Dinton, Wiltshire SP3 5EU.**

Tel: +44 (0)1722 716 376 Fax: +44 (0)1722 716 881
e-mail: sales@francisfrith.co.uk **www.francisfrith.com**